A Look at Vietnam

by Helen Frost

Consulting Editor: Gail Saunders-Smith, Ph.D.

Consultant: Christoph Giebel, Ph.D.
Professor of Southeast Asian History
and Vietnamese Studies
University of Washington

Pebble Books

an imprint of Capstone Press
Mankato, Minnesota

Pebble Books are published by Capstone Press
151 Good Counsel Drive, P.O. Box 669, Mankato, Minnesota 56002
www.capstonepress.com

1 2 3 4 5 6 07 06 05 04 03 02

Library of Congress Cataloging-in-Publication Data
Frost, Helen, 1949–
   A look at Vietnam / by Helen Frost.
   p. cm.—(Our world)
   Summary: Photographs and simple text present Vietnam, including its
geography, people, animals, and activities of daily life.
   Includes bibliographical references and index.
   ISBN-13: 978-0-7368-1431-7 (hardcover)
   ISBN-10: 0-7368-1431-0 (hardcover)
   ISBN-13: 978-0-7368-4854-1 (softcover pbk.)
   ISBN-10: 0-7368-4854-1 (softcover pbk.)
   1. Vietnam—Juvenile literature. [1. Vietnam.] I. Title. II. Series.
DS557.7 .F78 2003
959.7—dc21
                                                          2001007771

Note to Parents and Teachers

The Our World series supports national social studies standards related to culture. This book describes and illustrates the land, animals, and people of Vietnam. The images support early readers in understanding the text. The repetition of words and phrases helps early readers learn new words. This book also introduces early readers to subject-specific vocabulary words, which are defined in the Words to Know section. Early readers may need assistance to read some words and to use the Table of Contents, Words to Know, Read More, Internet Sites, and Index/Word List sections of the book.

Table of Contents

Hanoi
★

Vietnam

N
W ◀━━━▶ E
S

Vietnam is a country
in Southeast Asia. Vietnam
is shaped like the letter S.
The capital of Vietnam
is Hanoi.

Vietnam's flag

mountains

lowlands

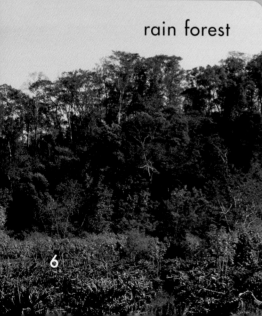

rain forest

river delta

6

Most of Vietnam has
a tropical climate. Vietnam
has mountains, lowlands,
rain forests, and river deltas.

monkey

water buffaloes

Monkeys live in Vietnam's rain forests. Water buffaloes in Vietnam sometimes take mud baths.

More than 78 million people live in Vietnam. Most people live near river deltas. Some people live in the mountains.

market in Hanoi, Vietnam

Vietnamese is the official language of Vietnam. Some people in Vietnam also speak Chinese, English, and Russian.

People in Vietnam shop in outdoor markets. Some markets are on boats. Some artists in Vietnam make crafts from wood and cloth.

fish market in Hoi An, Vietnam

Some workers in Vietnam make cars. Others fish or mine to earn money. Farmers grow rice, vegetables, and fruit.

Vietnam's money
is counted in dong.

Many people in Vietnam travel by bicycle. They also travel by motorcycle, boat, bus, and train.

Puppet shows are popular in Vietnam. Water puppets move on water. Shadow puppets seem to dance on a screen.

Words to Know

capital—the city in a country where the government is based; Hanoi is the capital of Vietnam; about 3 million people live in Hanoi.

delta—an area of land shaped like a triangle where a river enters a sea or ocean

language—the words and grammar that people use to talk and write to each other

market—a place where people can buy food and other items

popular—liked or enjoyed by many people

puppet—a toy in the shape of a person or an animal; a person controls the puppet by pulling strings or sticks that are attached to it or by moving his or her hand inside it.

rain forest—a thick area of trees where rain falls almost every day

tropical—an area that is hot and rainy

water buffalo—a black buffalo with long, curved horns

Read More

Kalman, Bobbie. *Vietnam: The Land.* The Lands, Peoples, and Cultures Series. New York: Crabtree Publishing, 2002.

Merrick, Patrick. *Vietnam.* Faces and Places. Chanhassen, Minn.: Child's World, 2000.

O'Connor, Karen. *Vietnam.* A Ticket to. Minneapolis: Carolrhoda Books, 1999.

Internet Sites

Kid's Eye on Asia Presents Vietnam
http://stmnftsc.melb.catholic.edu.au/
home/kidseyes/vietnam

Learn about Vietnam
http://www.vietnamembassy-usa.org/learn

Lonely Planet: Vietnam
http://www.lonelyplanet.com/
destinations/south_east_asia/vietnam

Index/Word List

Word Count: 163
Early-Intervention Level: 17

Editorial Credits

Mari C. Schuh, editor; Kia Adams, series designer; Jennifer Schonborn and Patrick D. Dentinger, book designers and illustrators; Alta Schaffer, photo researcher

Photo Credits

Christoph Giebel, 17
Corbis/Steve Raymer, 6 (upper right); Nik Wheeler, 6 (upper left); Neil Rabinowitz, 8 (bottom); Robert Maass, 12
Dave G. Houser/Houserstock, 18
Index Stock Imagery/Fred Scribner, cover
International Stock/Gerald Brimacombe, 1
John Elk III, 6 (bottom right), 20
One Mile Up, Inc., 5
Photri-Microstock, 8 (top)
Trip/A. Ghazzal, 10; T. Bognar, 14; Ask Images, 16
Wolfgang Kaehler/www.wkaehlerphoto.com, 6 (bottom left)